BRIGHT · SPARKS

Changes

by
Rosie Dalzell

Photographs: Zul Mukhida

Series Consultant: Sue Dale Tunnicliffe

CHERRYTREE BOOKS

A Cherrytree Book

Devised and produced by
Touchstone Publishing Ltd,
68 Florence Road, Brighton,
East Sussex BN1 6DJ

First published 1992
by Cherrytree Press Ltd
a subsidiary of
The Chivers Company Ltd,
Windsor Bridge Road,
Bath, Avon BA2 3AX

Copyright © Cherrytree Press Ltd 1992 and
Touchstone Publishing Ltd 1992

British Library Cataloguing in Publication data
Dalzell, Rosemary
 Changes. - (Bright sparks)
 I. Title II. Series
 574

 ISBN 0-7451-5139-6

Printed and bound by
Proost N.V., Turnhout, Belgium

All rights reserved. No part of this publication may be reproduced, stored in a retrieval system, or transmitted, in any form or by any means, without the prior permission in writing of the copyright holders, nor be otherwise circulated in any form of binding or cover other than that in which it is published and without a similar condition including this condition being imposed on the subsequent purchaser.

Contents

Projects

Giant ice ball 4
Dissolving race 6
Magic cabbage colours 8
Grating and grinding 10
Fizzy fountain 12
Coloured currents 14
Rust it! 16
Crystal collection 18
Tie and dye it! 20
Whisk it white! 22
Hard as rock? 24

Words to remember .. 26
Books to read 27
Places to go 27
More sparky ideas 28
Index 31

Words

Difficult **words** are explained on page 26.

Check

Before you start any project, check to see if there is a safety note (marked **!**) in the text. This means you need an adult to help you.

Giant ice ball

Ian's balloon is full of water. To fill a balloon like this, slip the neck over the end of a tap and turn it on.

Sophie knotted the top of her balloon and put it in the freezer for a day and a night. Try this yourself. What happens to the water? Tear off the balloon and see.

Look for bubbles in your ice ball. Can you see crystals? Will the ice ball float in a big bowl of water? What happens if you put salt on it?

! **Put the balloon in a plastic bag before freezing it.**

◀ **Freezing cold weather has turned the water that was flowing in this pipe into solid ice.**

Dissolving race

Stir a spoonful of sugar into a cup of water. What happens to the sugar? Taste the water and find out! Sugar **dissolves** in water.

What sort of sugar dissolves fastest – lumps, boiled sweets or fine sugar? Have a race with some friends and see. Each person needs a different type of sugar.

Leila, Nicky and Laurie filled their cups with water to the same level before they had their race. Why? What other things need to be the same to make it a fair test?

▶ **Sea-water contains dissolved salt. In hot sunshine the water dries off and leaves the salt behind. Here it is being collected.**

Magic cabbage colours

Tear up some red cabbage and put it in a bowl. Pour on hot water. What happens to the colour in the cabbage? Later, pour the water into a jug. What colour is it now?

Rachel is adding bicarbonate of soda to some of her cabbage water. Do the same. What happens? Try adding other liquids and powders to more cabbage water. Start by testing fruit juices and egg white.

Which things turn the water pink? They are **acids**. Which things turn it green or blue? They are **alkalis**.

◀ **The liquid in the bottle is an** indicator, **like your cabbage water. It shows if the soil is acid or alkaline.**

Grating and grinding

Laurie's heaps of crumbs are made from four different foods – toast, biscuit and two types of cereal. Which crumbs come from which food? Laurie is getting Nicky to taste the crumbs without looking, and guess.

Play the game with a friend. Think of other foods to crush, grate or grind into little pieces. What can you use to do this? There are some ideas in the picture.

! Ask an adult what foods you may use, and put them on a clean surface.

▶ **These African women are pounding grains of corn, crushing them to make flour.**

Fizzy fountain

Rachel is making things fizz! She has put some bicarbonate of soda in a bottle. Now she is adding vinegar, which is an acid.

Try this yourself. Then give your bottle a shake. What can you see in the liquid?

When the bicarbonate of soda and acid mix, they make a gas. Can you see any other acids in the picture? In a jar, mix an acid with another **carbonate**, such as egg shell or kettle scale. Look closely. What do you see?

◀ **Rachel has an upset stomach. This medicine contains an acid and a carbonate, so when you add it to water, it fizzes. It will make her feel better.**

Coloured currents

Make an ink-spout like Leila's. Find a small jar with a screw-on lid. Ask an adult to help you make two holes in the lid.

Put some food colouring in the jar and fill it to the top with hot water. Screw the lid on tightly. Gently lower the jar into a large jug of cold water – and watch.

Why do you think the coloured water moves upwards? After a time, what happens to the layer of colour?

▶ **The hang-glider flies on** currents **of hot air which sweep up from the warm valley to the cool hilltops.**

15

Rust it!

What makes things rust or **corrode**? Rachel set up four tests to find out. She put water in one box and salty water in another. The third box she kept dry. On the plate she put a damp cloth.

Next she sandpapered a patch on the empty food cans. Then she put a can, steel wool and nails in each box and on the plate, and left them for a week. What do you think happened? Try Rachel's experiment and see.

One of Rachel's boxes contains salty water. Which one?

◀ Air and water have corroded this copper roof, covering the shiny metal with a green powdery layer.

Crystal collection

Look closely at some sugar or salt. Can you see the tiny **crystals?** Laurie has grown some crystals from **borax**.

He put hot water in a cup and added borax. He stirred and added borax until no more would dissolve and some of it was left in the water. Then he put in food colouring, hung a string from a pencil and left the cup to cool.

Grow some crystals for yourself. As well as borax, you could try Epsom salts, citric acid, alum or table salt.

▶ **These** mineral **crystals have formed** naturally in rocks. The purple ones are amethyst.

Tie and dye it!

Sophie and Ian are making **dyes** from fruits and leaves. Ian is adding water to spinach to make his dye. What could he do to help the colour dissolve in the water?

Sophie mashed berries in hot water to make her dye. She poured her mixture through a strainer into the bowl.

Find some white cloth and make a dye to colour it. You could tie marbles in the cloth first. What happens? Try adding salt to the dye. Does it work better?

! **If you need to heat things up, ask an adult to help.**

◀ **Modern dyes can be made in strong, bright colours, like those being used here to print cloth.**

Whisk it white!

Break an egg on to a plate and throw away the shell. Try Hannah's way of trapping the yolk as the white runs into a bowl. Is it really white? Can you see through it?

Beat your egg white with a whisk, as Lawrence is doing. How has the egg white changed? Tiny air bubbles are caught in it.

Ask an adult to help you make meringues with your fluffy egg white. In the oven, the heat changes the egg white so that it hardens around the trapped air.

▶ **Rachel is whisking egg whites and yolks together to make a sponge cake. Find out what other things you can change by whisking.**

Hard as rock?

Are all **rocks** hard? Collect different rocks and find out by scraping them with a blunt knife. Ian is testing sandstone. Will hard rocks scratch softer ones? Can you make a mark on paper with any of your rocks?

Chalk is a type of rock called limestone. Try Sophie's experiment. Shake a piece of chalk in one jar, and chalk and water in another (leave some air in it). Look at the chalk. What happens to limestone in wind and rain?

! **Only shake chalk in a jar – not other rocks.**

◀ **Sea-water has washed against these sandstone rocks and worn them away.**

24

Words to remember

Acid A substance that turns red cabbage indicator pink and reacts with carbonates to make a gas.
Alkali A substance that turns red cabbage indicator blue or green – the opposite of an acid.
Borax White crystals used in washing clothes.
Carbonate A substance that reacts with an acid to make carbon dioxide gas.
Corrode A metal corrodes when it reacts with the air. When iron or steel corrode, they slowly change into a reddish-brown, crumbly substance called rust.
Crystal A shiny piece of solid, often transparent, with a regular shape, sharp edges and flat surfaces.
Current A stream of air or water.
Dissolve To mix something with a liquid so that it disappears into the liquid.
Dye A substance that will change the colour of cloth or other things.
Indicator Something that shows by its colour whether another substance is an acid or an alkali.
Minerals Pure crystals in the earth's surface from which we get all our metals and many other chemicals.
Rocks The mixtures of minerals that make up the crust, or surface layer, of the earth.

Books for you

Caves and *Icebergs* by Jenny Wood (Two-Can)
First Usborne Book of Science by Gaby Waters (Usborne)
My Science Book of Air and *My Science Book of Water* by Neil Ardley (Dorling Kindersley)

Books to look at with an adult

Rock and Mineral by Bob Symes (Dorling Kindersley)
Take Nobody's Word For It by George Auckland and Bill Coates (BBC Books)
Amazing Air by Henry Smith (Walker Books)
Liquid Magic by Philip Watson (Walker Books)
Rocks and Fossils by Martyn Bramwell (Usborne)

Places to go

Buxton Micrarium, The Crescent, Buxton, Derbyshire SK17 6BQ. Watch crystals growing under a huge microscope.
The Natural History Museum, Earth Galleries (formerly the Geological Museum), Exhibition Road, London SW7 2DE
Techniquest, 72 Bute Street, Cardiff CF1 6AA.
The Exploratory, The Old Station, Temple Meads, Bristol BS1 6QU.

More sparky ideas

Here are some background facts, things to look out for and ideas for more experiments.

pp 4-5 Giant ice ball
● The ice ball will be bigger than the original balloon of water because water expands as it solidifies (most materials contract). If water in a pipe freezes in winter it will expand and may break the pipe.
● Because of this expansion, ice is less dense than water and floats on it.
● Salt lowers the melting point of ice. A small heap of it will form a melting crater on your ice ball.

pp 6-7 Dissolving race
● Solids dissolve faster if they are broken up into small particles or stirred or heated.
● To make the race fair, everyone should ideally use the same amount of sugar (you could weigh the sweets and sugar), add it to water of the same temperature and start stirring at the same time.
● To show that dissolving is not the same as melting, heat some sugar very gently in a saucepan until it melts. Put it in a tin and let it cool and solidify again.

pp 8-9 Magic cabbage colours
● The cabbage colour dissolves in the water to make an indicator.
● Common acids include fruit juices, vinegar, cream of tartar and fizzy drinks. Bicarbonate of soda, egg white, washing soda and ammonia are all alkalis.
● Add an alkali slowly to a cup of cabbage water and acid. Try to find the neutral point (purple).

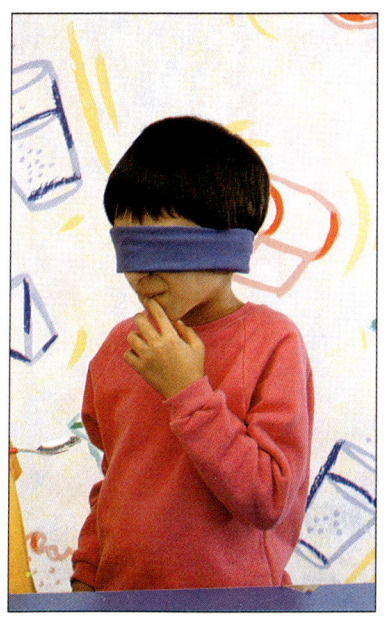

pp 10-11 Grating and grinding
- The four foods are all made from cereals, so, reduced to small particles, they look and taste very similar.
- Make fruit milk-shakes and colour them unlikely colours. Can your friends guess which fruit is in each?

pp 12-13 Fizzy fountain
- Carbonates react with acids, neutralizing them and making carbon dioxide (the gas which makes the fizz in fizzy drinks). Try adding cabbage water to this experiment. It should slowly change colour.
- Baking powder is a mixture of an acid and bicarbonate of soda. In wet cake mixture the two slowly react, making carbon dioxide gas which helps cakes to rise.

pp 14-15 Coloured currents
- Most things expand as they get hot, and this makes them lighter (less dense). So the hot coloured water rises to the surface, cools, sinks, and more hot water flows up from the jar. These movements, called convection currents, can form in any gas or liquid, including air.
- Gliders, hot-air balloons and gliding birds are carried up by currents of warm air.

pp 16-17 Rust it!
- Iron reacts with the oxygen and water in air to make rust. In dry air, or a sealed container of boiled water, iron will not rust.
- Other common metals corrode, too, but either more slowly (silver) or just on the outside (copper).
- Salt makes iron corrode faster.
- Because iron can rust right through, it is often covered with a protective layer – paint, plastic, zinc (galvanizing), tin or oil. Scratching the tin surface on iron cans lets that part rust more easily.

29

pp 18-19 Crystal collection
● You can buy citric acid, borax, alum and Epsom salts from most chemist's shops.
● Crystals are formed when the particles in a solid fit together in a regular way to make geometric shapes.
● Water particles are often included in the crystal pattern, so coloured water can make coloured crystals. An exception is cubic salt crystals.
● Gemstones, such as amethysts, diamonds, rubies and emeralds, are all natural mineral crystals.

pp 20-21 Tie and dye it!
● To help the spinach dye dissolve in the water you could cut the leaves into smaller pieces, heat them up with the water and stir or mash them (see **Dissolving race**).
● Salt helps dye stick to cloth. Cotton is the best material to use. Boiling it in the dye for a few minutes also helps to fix the colour.

pp 22-23 Whip it white!
● The protein in egg white is changed by whipping (or heating) and becomes an opaque solid.
● Unusually for a food, egg white is alkaline (see **Magic cabbage colours**). Try adding a little acid, cream of tartar or vinegar. It also helps the protein coagulate.

pp 24-25 Hard as rock?
● The hardest rocks are formed deep inside the earth, where the temperature and pressure are very high.
● Weather slowly wears down or dissolves rocks and washes them to the sea as sand and mud. This gradually turns into soft rocks, such as sandstone.
● Other soft rocks formed at the earth's surface include chalk, made from the skeletons of tiny sea creatures; coal, from ancient forests; and rock salt from evaporated seas.

Index

acids 8, 12
air 14, 16, 24
alkalis 8

carbonates 12
chalk 24
cloth 20
colours 14, 18, 20
corroding 16
crystals 18
currents 14

dissolving 6, 18, 20
dyes 20

fizzing 12
floating 4
freezing 4

gas 12
grating 10

hang-glider 14
heating 22

ice 4
indicator 8

limestone 24

minerals 18

rocks 24
rust 16

salt 4, 6, 18, 20
salty water 16
sandstone 24
sugar 6, 18

whisking 22

Thank you!

The author and publishers would like to thank junior scientists Alice, Ben, Charlie, Christopher, Emily, Francesca, Joanna, Maxim and Oliver for their work on the experiments; and Hannah, Lawrence, Rachel, Ian, Sophie, Laurie, Leila and Nicky for appearing in the photographs.

Thanks also to the staff of St Bartholomew's CE First School, Knoll Infants School, Queens Park First School and Balfour First School, all of Brighton and Hove, for their co-operation.

The author would also like to thank Hugh, Thomas, Kate and Harry for all their help and encouragement.

Credits

The projects were devised and set up by the author. The studio photographs are all by Zul Mukhida, with backgrounds by Maureen Jackson. Other pictures were supplied by: Eye Ubiquitous (Thelma Sanders), p.10; David Cumming, p.16; Natural History Museum, p.18; Science Photo Library (Vaughan Fleming), p.4; Science Photo Library (Guy Gillette), p.20; ZEFA (J. Behnke), p.6; ZEFA, p.14; Zul Colour Library,

This book is to be returned on or before the last date below.

574   C034283

DALZELL, ROSIE

CHANGES

HAVERING SCHOOL LIBRARY SERVICE